Bible Verse Addictions

Cause and Effect
(Volume Two)

Gregory Madison

AWE OF MY LIFE
PUBLICATIONS
AWE IN AWE

Bible Verses Addictions- Cause and Effect Volume 2

Copyright © 2018 by Gregory Madison

AWE OF MY LIFE PUBLICATIONS
www.turningtoGodfromidols.com

Originally printed on Madison's Bible Verses Additions
Facebook page

Library of Congress Cataloging-in-Publication Data
Madison, Gregory
Bible Verses Addictions- Cause and Effect

978-0-9701209-3-9

Turned to God from Idols
By Gregory Madison

As I look back over my life, it is hard to believe that I was hooked on crack for 23 years. During that time, I participated in both Christian and secular programs (at least 14 or 15.) The programs included Veteran facilities, Pacific Garden Mission in Chicago, a farm program in Colorado (owned by Denver Rescue Mission), as well as many others. Very early during my struggle with my addiction to crack (and the other addictions that went with it), I sought to discover what the Bible has to say concerning addictions. In 1996, I began a personal study describing the link between addiction and idolatry. This is now a lifetime study.

Although I had begun to find the answers that I was looking for concerning addictions, I kept going back to using. During those 23 years, the longest time that I remained sober was for 17 months (mainly because I lived away from the city, at that time.) I lived in different places for 7 years, going from one program to another. At other times, I lived on the streets and with friends (on and off drugs.) It was in the year 2003 that I decided that there was no way that I was ever going to quit using drugs again. This was the first time that I had ever stooped to that level. Since I had made such a decision, I thought that it would be best for me to go to Florida where I could find what is thought to be the purest cocaine.

After spending the winter in Florida and going back north in the summer for two years, I returned to Cleveland, Ohio. Somehow, God began to convince me that His way is best and that my actions were highly offensive towards He and my fellowman. I thought of how I was not only depriving myself but also God (as well as others.) This led to a decision to remain in Cleveland and seek out the help of my family and the faith community. I vowed to never move away until I had thoroughly allowed God to deal with my addictions and was 'stable'. For about the next 6 years I went into the VA several times, joined different churches, and continued to read and write bible-based material on addictions.

From 2005 until 2011 I sought to develop a consistent life of sobriety. I would sometimes go for months at a time, only to return to drugs. In January of 2011, I heard that my grandmother in Memphis, Tennessee was very ill. I knew that I could be of no help to her (or anyone) because of the investments that I was making on my addictions. I started doing everything I needed to do so that I would be able to assist my grandmother and her husband (86 and 96, at the time) as soon as possible. Through the power of Christ, the strength of His Word, the prayers and support of my dad, and with the aid of a church as well as others, I was able to begin a consistent walk with Christ for 2 months before traveling to Memphis. One year after my first visit to Memphis, I moved there. And so now, the things that are most important to me are hearing God and being used by Him. True and lasting sobriety, <u>that is pleasing to God</u>, is found in Christ alone. To be continued…

Preface

Bible Verses Addictions is a play on words. What we really mean is the Bible versus addictions. The Bible confronts addictions at every point. The Bible presents the origin of addictions. The Bible exposes the true nature of addictions. The Bible explains addictions activities (dynamics.) The Bible explains the consequences of addiction. And, of course, the Bible gives us the solution to addiction, like no other source. The Bible *even* offers an alternative to addictions.

The Lord said that man shall not live on bread alone, but on every word that proceeds out of the mouth of God. As bread addresses and attacks the physical hunger, the Word of God addresses and attacks the spiritual hunger that some of us try to fill with an addiction.

A deeper study of the Word of God for addicts answers the question asked by Dr. Edward T. Welch in his illustrious book *Addictions: A Banquet in the Grave.*

> **"Do you have a good grasp on the wealth of biblical material that speaks precisely to the modern problems of addictions? Can you go through any book in scripture, even if it doesn't mention alcohol, food, or sex, and see how it speaks to addictions?"**

While talking with a friend, I was very much encouraged when he told me that although the program that he was in was of a secular nature, God has been blessing him with a remembrance of Scripture while sitting in the groups that he is required to attend, so that he can benefit from the housing and employment opportunities that the program has to offer. Suddenly, God reminded me of the Hebrew boys in Babylon who refused to eat the king's meat. I saw this as a symbol of the secular program that my friend was forced to participate in. In fact, as he told me about one of the "defilements" that the program embraces, and we both agreed upon its falsehood.

A well-known quote of the group my friend had to participate in is that "the Bible saves your soul; this program saves your behind." Well, my friend and I both agreed that the Bible can save your behind as well as your soul. And besides, I could see how much better off my friend is (just as the Hebrew boys) with the program that God has implemented long before any of these secular programs were even dreamed of (established by the blood of Christ and administered to us through the blessed Holy Spirit, initiated and performed by His Word.) Again, I will say, until my dying day, **"the highest form of sobriety known unto mankind is in Jesus Christ."**

Introduction

One thing that I want to make perfectly clear, from the very start, is that **Bible Verses Addictions** is intended to apply to any and every addiction. Whether we are addicted to drugs, pornography, gambling, overeating… the Word of God is more than adequate for guidance.

> *All scripture is given by inspiration of God, and is <u>profitable</u> for doctrine, for reproof, for correction, for instruction in righteousness.*
> **2 Timothy 3:16 KJV**

In an article that is titled "The Distinguishing Feature of Christian Counseling", Dr. Wayne A. Mack says that **"Christ-centered counseling involves understanding the nature and courses of our human difficulties, understanding the ways we are unlike Christ in our values, aspirations, desires, thoughts, feelings, choices, attitudes, actions, and responses. Resolving those sin-related difficulties includes being redeemed and justified through Christ, receiving God's forgiveness through Christ, and acquiring from Christ the enabling power to replace unChristlike**

(sinful) patterns of life with Christlike, godly ones." This is what is found in a biblical approach to addictions.

<u>First and foremost, a deeper study of the Word of God for an addict is an expression of the reverence one has for God.</u>

There are several questions that come to mind. Does the Word of God really have something to say about addictions?

If the Word of God did not have anything to say about addictions, then God would not have created us!

To think of God as the kind of God that has created us but does not give us the instructions that we need to survive, and even prosper and be at peace, is an irreverent and distorted view of God. Here is yet another question for us to consider! Is God worthy of being heard? Who would dare say no? I, also, must ask, **do we care enough about people to give them the very best**?

<u>Our reverence for God is demonstrated by how we extend ourselves to those who were created in His image</u>.

My attitude is as the apostle Paul's, who said, "I kept back nothing that was profitable unto you" (Acts 20:20). There is no better way to expose and dispose of addictions except through the Word of God. The Word of God is the truth, addictions are but lies. So, why not give people the very best? Not only that, true sobriety, restoration, recovery, sanctification … is built upon a healthy reverence for God.

There are only three basic reasons why people turn from addictions.

1. To avoid the consequences behind addictions.
2. To reap the benefits of abstinence.
3. Out of reverence for God.

Reverence for God leads us to the Word of God to deal with addictions. This, in turn, leads us to a reverence for God as being the first principle of concern in resolving the issue of addiction (as well as anything else.)

And so, first, God is worthy of telling us His view on addictions.

Another reason for a deeper study of the Word of God for addicts is to build up their faith. We who have been in the habit of putting our trust in an addiction, need to develop and maintain faith in God. Faith comes by hearing and hearing by the Word of God (Romans 10:17). As quiet as it is kept (though some may deny it) addicts have a small view of God. Addicts have trouble seeing how good God is. Addicts don't understand how merciful and forgiving God is. Addicts have trouble believing that God has all power. It is because of this deficiency of faith that people lean upon their own understanding and put their trust in idolatrous addictions.

The written Word of God gives us the most accurate description there is of God. **The most vivid description of God is found in the living Word of God (Jesus Christ, also described in the written Word of God.)** Another reason why the addict needs to have their faith built up by studying the Word of God is so that they can be on one accord with God as they pray.

> *A deeper study of the Word of God discloses and eradicates the deception and error on which addictions are rooted. Three basic areas of deceit that give addictions their strength is; the misinformation that they give concerning God, concerning ourselves, and the addiction (itself.)*

Addictions discredit God. Addiction, basically, tell us that God is not to be trusted,

He doesn't love us all that much, He doesn't know what He is talking about, we don't have to answer to Him (and many other lies if we were to really think about it.) The lies that are behind addictions concerning ourselves is that we know what is best, we are not all that bad, we can handle it (and again, many, many lies.)

Addictions deceive us into thinking that they can fulfill our lives, they are harmless (or at least don't cause much harm), we could never be under their control … Jesus said that if we continue in His word then we will know the truth, and the truth would make us free (John 8:32). The deception behind addictions are dispelled as the Spirit of Truth (the Holy Spirit) applies the word of truth to our lives.

A deeper study of the Word of God provides us with the greatest alternative to addictions. It is in the study of God's Word that we discover and practice the highest and purest motive behind our abstinence. That motive of remaining abstinent that surpasses any other is simply to love God. We love God because He first loved us. We don't know just how much He loves us apart from His Word. We love God as we cling to and embrace His Word. We love God as we converse with Him through His Word. We love Him as we obey His Word. As we embrace the things of God, the things of the world lose their grip. We delight in the Word of God rather than the things of the world.

No one can serve two masters. Either you will hate the one and love the other, or you will be devoted to the one and despise the other.
Matthew 6:24a

Praise the Lord. Blessed are those who fear the Lord, who find great delight in his commands.
Psalms 112:1

If ye then be risen with Christ, seek those things which are above, where Christ sitteth on the right hand of God. Set your affection on things above, not on things on the earth. For ye are dead, and your life is hid with Christ in God.
Colossians 3:1-3

The alternative to loving God leads us to put on the Lord Jesus Christ. Putting on the Lord Jesus Christ involves being concerned with others as He was. Putting on Christ, also, means that we rely upon His power, His strength and His wisdom to make it through the difficulties of life (including the temptations of addiction.) Most importantly, ***putting on Christ provides us with the highest level of sobriety known to man***.

A deeper study of the Word of God teaches us how to help others as well. A study of God's Word teaches those who have succumb to addictions to repent from living such a self-absorbed life that they are of no good to others. As we study the Word of God, we are granted closer fellowship with others who do the same. A regular study of the Word of God causes us to become more skillful in its use and thereby being of greater aid to others.

To know the Word of God is to know the mind of God and thereby able to give sound advice to others. The Spirit of God teaches our hands to war (Ps. 18:34), with the Sword of the Spirit (the Word of God, Eph. 6: 17), so that we may be able to restore others. The Word of God instructs us on our relationship with others. The Word of God gives wisdom.

If we do not look to the Word of God for answers to addictions and rely upon other sources alone, we are acting irreverently towards God.

a. We are saying that God doesn't know enough- He's a fool
b. We are saying that God doesn't care enough- He is evil and can't be trusted
c. We are saying that God doesn't have enough power- He is weak and sorry

d. We are saying that we don't care what God has to say- I've got all the answers
e. We are saying that we don't mind on taking a chance of being deceived
f. We are saying that God doesn't have the right to tell me what to do

A Deeper Study of the Word of God on Addictions

1. A matter of reverence for God
2. Builds faith in God
a. Addicts tend to have a small view of God
(1) God is good
(2) God offer's forgiveness
(3) God has all power

b. Being on one accord with God/providing communion with God
(1) God speaks
(2) Grounds for praying according to the will of God

3. Dispels deception and error
a. About God
b. About oneself
c. About addiction/sin

4. Provides an alternative to the addiction
a. Proper motives for sobriety
b. Putting on Christ

5. Teaches how to help others
a. Provides wisdom
b. The Sword of the Spirit (also, James 5:19f.)

Cause

We praise what we worship
The will of God
Aroma
Choices
Cleaving
Addictions 101
House rules
Plain and simple
Like a mother
Starting point
Conviction
Cleansing and healing (1-3)
I, being of a sound mind (1-2)
The mistaken identity
Are you an addict (1-3)?
Captivated
Integrity battles discontentment

The cause of addiction lies within its definition. The attractiveness that these idols pretend to offer allurement for us outside of the influence of God. The statements below are not in any order and are not an exhaustive list of the causes behind addictions. They are, however, enough for one to gain a good understanding of the nature and origin, the power and effects of addictions.

We Praise What We Worship

> *You shall fear the Lord your God; you
> shall serve Him, and to Him you shall hold
> fast, and take oaths in His name. He is
> your praise, and He is your God, who has
> done for you these great and awesome
> things which your eyes have seen.*
> *Deuteronomy 10:20-21*

**That which we praise is often in our
thoughts and conversation.**

We have good thoughts and we speak well of
that which we praise. During my years of drug
treatment, I would often hear people being told
to be careful not to glorify their addiction
(while sharing their experiences.)

I like eating. Eating is such a big thing for
me that when I started getting bigger, my dad
said that if I continued to eat as much as I did,
that I would have to learn to cook and buy the
food myself. Thus, my cooking career began.
(Don't worry, I'm blessed with a high
metabolism and don't gain weight easily.) **Food
is important to me. I think about it. I speak
well of it. If I am not careful, it becomes my
praise.** I have noticed that my wife and I talk
about food a lot. Yet another reason for fasting
when addressing our addictions (forgive me for
not going into detail!)

In one of the most recent sermons that I have listened to, the speaker said that whatever you fear is your God. One of the dynamics of an addiction is to be under its influence. That which we fear influences us, just as that which is our praise.

The Will of God

But He said to me, "My grace is sufficient for you, for my power is made perfect in weakness." Therefore I will boast all the more gladly about my weaknesses, so that Christ's power may rest on me.
2 Corinthians 12:9

Last week, I corrected a man for saying something that I have been guilty of saying myself. When the man said that we have had enough rain, I told him that only God knows how much is enough, we just think that we know.

One thing that we can all agree on about addictions is that they thrive on and embrace comfort and ease.

So long as our addictions give us pleasure, we're "good." I once heard someone wisely say that temptations look good but are not good for us, and trials don't look good but they are good for us.

Psalms 15:4 commends the person who "sweareth to his own hurt". Persistence, integrity, humility, and growth are just a few of the characteristics that are channeled and developed through pain and suffering. And, guess what? We cannot get around it! That's life!

> *Yet man is born to trouble as surely as sparks fly upward **Job 5:7***

And, if you are a child of God, through Christ, you are going to suffer. Why suffer in addition by engaging in an addiction? Someone once said to me that **life has enough problems, "why add to them?"** In case you are not convinced that you are going to suffer as a child of God, I will cite just 2 verses that say so.

> *To this you were called, because Christ suffered for you, leaving you*

*an example, that you should follow
in his steps. **1 Peter 2:21***

*Endure hardship as discipline; God
is treating you as his children. For
what children are not disciplined by
their father? **Hebrews 12:7 (read
vv. 7-10)***

One of the tools that have been used for
support groups is the "Serenity Prayer". I think
that it is best used when it is quoted in its
entirety (of which most are not familiar with.)

GOD, grant me the serenity
to accept the things
I cannot change,
Courage to change the
things I can, and the
wisdom to know the difference.
Living one day at a time;
Enjoying one moment at a time;
Accepting hardship as the
pathway to peace.
Taking, as He did, this
sinful world as it is,
not as I would have it.
Trusting that He will make
all things right if I
surrender to His Will;

That I may be reasonably happy
in this life, and supremely
happy with Him forever in
the next.

Amen

Aroma

*Then Jesus declared, "I am the bread of life.
Whoever comes to me will never go hungry,
and whoever believes in me will never be
thirsty.* **John 6:35**

Just the other day, as I was talking with a man
about a bakery that was being demolished, he
began reminiscing over his past delight of
smelling freshly baked bread while the bakery
was in operation.

**Addiction stink! They stink to
high heaven (literally!!!)
Addictions stink in the nostrils
of God. And, so long as our
senses are in working order,
they stink in our nostrils as well.**

There is nothing foul in the aroma that Christ gives. As the bread of life, he is completely appetizing.

Have you ever heard someone say, "Something just doesn't smell right" when they are about to engage in a certain matter? Addictions can easily dull our senses. I am reminded of two illustrations that apply to this.

> 1. If you place a frog in a pot of water that is room temperature and put the pot on the stove, gradually heating the water until it boils, the frog will boil to death before noticing the change of temperature. **We are all vulnerable to sin in this same fashion.**

> 2. It is said that when Eskimos want to kill a wolf that has been eating the seals that the Eskimos want for themselves, the Eskimos prey off the wolf's senses. Knowing how bloodthirsty the wolf is, the Eskimos plant a sharp knife in the ice-coated with seal's blood and wait for the wolf to come lick the blade so that the wolf cuts his tongue. The wolf becomes so frantic over the taste of blood that he does not even realize that he is licking his own blood after a

> while and eventually bleeds to
> death. This is how we are with
> addictions.

Death is one thing that both illustrations have in common. Indulging in addictions lead to death (whether physical death, spiritual death, the death of a relationship, our senses go dead...) And, it is a known fact that death stinks. The smell of death is not hard to miss. Not only that, the smell of death spreads. So, it is with Christ also! Jesus gives a distinguishable aroma (just like the unmistakable aroma of the bread at the bakery.) And not only that, Jesus spreads that same aroma to his followers.

> *But thanks be to God, who always leads us as captives in Christ's triumphal procession and uses us to spread the aroma of the knowledge of him everywhere. For we are to God the pleasing aroma of Christ among those who are being saved and those who are perishing. To the one we are an aroma that brings death; to the other, an aroma that brings life. And who is equal to such a task?* **2 Corinthians 2:14-16**

Choices

*Now when you hear the sound of the horn,
flute, zither, lyre, harp, pipe and all kinds
of music, if you are ready to fall down and
worship the image I made, very good. But if
you do not worship it, you will be thrown
immediately into a blazing furnace. Then
what god will be able to rescue you from my
hand?" Daniel 3:15*

**Addictions blurt out empty threats as
Nebuchadnezzar did to the three Hebrew
boys. Satan would have us to believe that we
have no other choice than to bow down to
addictions. He wants us to deny the power of
God**. But, just as the Hebrews, <u>we can be
confident that God cares, God knows, God is
living and active, God is all-powerful, and yes,
He is with us amidst our trials and temptations,
through Christ</u>.

Cleaving

*That thou mayest love the Lord thy God,
and that thou mayest obey His voice, and
that thou mayest cleave unto Him: for He
is thy life, and the length of thy days: that*

> *thou mayest dwell in the land which the*
> *Lord sware unto thy fathers, to Abraham,*
> *to Isaac, and to Jacob, to give them.*
> ***Deuteronomy 30:20***

> *Nevertheless he cleaved unto the sins of*
> *Jeroboam the son of Nebat, which made*
> *Israel to sin; he departed not therefrom.*
> ***2 Kings 3:3***

What a contrast we see in these two verses on cleaving! I would venture to say that the cleaving mentioned in 2 Kings would be the equivalent of an addiction! Jesus makes a clear distinction of our cleaving in Matthew 6:24.

> *No one can serve two masters; for*
> *either he will hate the one and love*
> *the other, or else he will be loyal to*
> *the one and despise the other. You*
> *cannot serve God and mammon.*

Addictions 101

*So God created man in His own image; in the image of God He created him; male and female He created them. **Genesis 1:27***

God created man in His own image. When mankind sided with Satan, we became like Satan. Here is a description of Satan:

> *"How you are fallen from heaven,*
> *O Lucifer, son of the morning!*
> *How you are cut down to the ground,*
> *You who weakened the nations!*
> *For you have said in your heart:*
> *'I will ascend into heaven,*
> *I will exalt my throne above the stars of God;*
> *I will also sit on the mount of the congregation*
> *On the farthest sides of the north;*
> *I will ascend above the heights of the clouds,*
> *I will be like the Most High.'*
> ***Isaiah 14:12-14***

Satan longs for power (to say the least.) Indulging in addiction is a quest for power as well. We long to have all power (which belongs to God alone.) In fact, we would just

as soon wipe God out in our addictions, just as Satan would. The Scripture, also, tells us that God is love. 1 Corinthians 13:4-7 gives us a description of love.

> *Love suffers long and is kind; love does not envy; love does not parade itself, is not puffed up; does not behave rudely, does not seek its own, is not provoked, thinks no evil; does not rejoice in iniquity, but rejoices in the truth; bears all things, believes all things, hopes all things, endures all things.*

From my experiences and observation, this does not resemble someone in pursuit of an addiction. From the 'fall' of man, we forsook the image of God. Right from birth, we are corrupt (to say the least.) But the good news is that <u>God has provided the one and only way for us have His image restored in us once again</u>. Thus, we have the familiar verse 2 Corinthians 5:17.

> *Therefore, if anyone is in Christ, he is a new creation; old things have passed away; behold, all things have become new.*

House Rules

The earth is the LORD's, and everything in it, the world, and all who live in it.
Psalm 24:1

This morning I thought about how it has been a while since my wife and I have babysat for a couple that we know at church. I thought about how we have had to explain some of the house rules to the children over the last year and a half that we have been honored with their presence. Then I thought about all the times that I had to stay in various shelters and other people's houses during my years of homelessness. **One of the 'coping skills' that I adopted was to remind myself that 'it ain't my house'.** I don't care where you go, who you stay with ... there is one rule that supersedes all others.

> *"The house rules" is the number one rule of any house, whether the rules that follow are reasonable or demanding, pleasant or harsh. Rule number one is that you recognize who rules, you give them honor, show them respect...*

We are all God's guests in this great big world that He owns. The house rules were given to Israel through Moses to pass on to the rest of the world and have now been placed in the hands of believers in Christ. God has told us that 'the house rules' by way of the first commandment given to Israel.

> *Thou shalt have no other gods before me. Exodus 20:3*

Most of us will admit that there are some things, which, we will not do around certain people. It seems that we have a certain amount of respect and consideration for these people. Some of us wouldn't dream of cursing in the presence of our parents. (Though this society is steeped in moral decadence) it would still be uncommon for a spouse to engage in adultery in the very presence of their mate. Yet, this is exactly what happens when people choose addiction over God.

Addictions are a form of idolatry. Idolatry, in turn, is spiritual adultery. No doubt about it, when we make an idol of something we are "cheating on God."

It is only as God is given ownership over this individual house (our body) that we are able to honor Him as He deserves. Unless you have been purchased by the blood of Christ, then you are still your own. That's why the attitude that many have concerning their actions is that they can do whatever they want, nobody owns them. True enough, but you don't own the whole world. It ain't your house! The House rules. Guess what! God is the House.

Plain and Simple

Therefore, since we have such hope, we use great boldness of speech. **2 Corinthians 3:12**

I was just talking with a friend yesterday about all the various titles that I have in my library on addictions. Most of which are from a biblical perspective. Yet and still, I must part with many of these because they are not plain enough in their deliberation. Don't get me wrong! I do not believe that they are of no use at all. Just like secular material, they are of some value. It's just that my focus on addictions are of a different nature (you might say.)

I love that way that the Word of God speaks about how the leaders of Israel communicated with the public.

> *So Ezra the priest brought the Law before the assembly of men and women and all who could hear with understanding.*
> **Nehemiah 8:1**

> *they read distinctly from the book, in the Law of God; and they gave the sense, and helped them to understand the reading.*
> ***Nehemiah 8:8***

Hebert Lockyer said, in *All the Divine Names and Titles of the Bible* that, "Because sin and unbelief have warped the mind of man, he is in constant need of guidance and advice from above (1 Kings 3:7-10). What a relief to know that there is a Counsellor able to answer our questions, solve our riddles, and relieve us of our perplexity!"

In the first place, if the material that I study or present does not present Christ in a major capacity it is an insult to God and not of the greatest use to others.

Secondly, I happen to believe that addictions are best described and treated (exposed and disposed of) as idols. It is here that the Scriptures are greatest of use. It is here that we are motivated to love God and not just to rid ourselves of the unpleasantries of addiction.

Like A Mother

"Can a woman forget her nursing child, that she should have no compassion on the son of her womb? Even these may forget, yet I will not forget you. Isaiah 49:15 ESV

I would be a fool if I failed to recognize the love that my wife has for her children although they were separated years ago because of a court decision due to the unstable environment of the spousal abuse my wife endured by her previous husband. I cannot deny the beauty and strength of a woman who still remembers her children the way that my wife does. I am grateful for the way that this only strengthens the relationship that we have with one another. And my wife is just as close to her children as she ever was in that her love has not changed.

Now, do you think that our love for idolatrous addiction changes God's love for us? Israel's idolatry did not change God's love for them. Alienation and estrangement are two words that are used by Edward T. Welch to describe addictions.

> *Arising out of our alienation from the Living God, addiction is bondage to the rule of a substance, activity, or state of*

> *mind, which then becomes the center of life, defending itself from the truth, and leading to further estrangement from God's kingdom.* -Addictions: A Banquet in the Grave

Get it straight! **Addictions don't change God's love for us, addictions change our love for God**. It is the result of us not seeing God properly. That's why I said that my wife's love for her children strengthens our relationship. There are things in my wife that I probably would not recognize and appreciate were it not for the love that she expresses for her children by way of reminiscence.

How we view God is a basic element when turning to God from idols. We do not gravitate to people and things that we do not find attractive in some form or fashion.

I was recently reminded of another mother I admired years ago. It was a shock to discover that a close acquaintance had not only got married but had also produced a son. I really loved the joy and glee of my friend's son as he interacted with his loving mother. The thing that really fascinated me was that it seemed as though **this boy's mother was the most beautiful woman in the world to him though**

the woman had a skin condition that most people would find unattractive. It was the love of that mother that gave the boy such joy and glee. (He was probably the happiest little boy I have ever met.)

The love of God is unimaginably more attractive than a mother's love. I am living proof that, in spite of our ugliness, God loves us. Calvary is the greatest proof.

> In this is love, not that we have loved God but that He loved us and sent His Son to be the propitiation for our sins. *1 John 4:10*

Starting point

> "For My thoughts are not your thoughts, Nor are your ways My ways," says the Lord. "For as the heavens are higher than the earth, So are My ways higher than your ways, And My thoughts than your thoughts." *Isaiah 55:8*

Isaiah 55 has some key phrases that help us to gain a greater understanding of God's perspective and guidance on addictions.

> "Ho! Everyone who thirsts (v.1)
>
> Why do you spend money for what is not bread,
> And your wages for what does not satisfy? (v.2)
>
> Seek the Lord while He may be found (v.6)
>
> Let the wicked forsake his way,
> And the unrighteous man his thoughts;
> Let him return to the Lord (v.7)

On the back cover of *Turning to God from Idols*, I stated that "the issue of addiction can be very complicating. The reason behind this is because you are dealing with something that is foreign. The element of addiction is an instrument of the devil. Dealing with an addiction can difficult because the devil is a liar and a deceiver.

We don't have the understanding that we need to please God and be on one accord with Him unless the understanding comes from Him. The understanding that we need is based on reasoning. God is not as stupid as some make Him out to be.

When God reasons with us we get a view of reality. With a proper reverence for God, we are able to see the reality of addictions. Be sure that you reverently build your foundation of sobriety on the reasoning that God has given in His Word, by His Holy Spirit!

Conviction

For my people have committed two evils; they have forsaken Me the fountain of living waters, and hewed them out cisterns, broken cisterns, that can hold no water.
Jeremiah 2:13

Our conviction leads us to the reality of two basic facts.

> 1. We have wronged God
> 2. We wrong ourselves wrong (as well as others)

Though God is forgiving, the first issue (offending God) should not be as lightly considered as most programs on addictions.

In fact, this is the general attitude of the day. **It has become so horrific that many times the issue of offending God is never**

mentioned as though we should not sin simply because it does us harm.

Passages like Jeremiah 2:13 should not be overlooked or taken lightly when addressing addictions. I was not aware of their enormity until being led in a study of the components of idolatry express in so many passages that coincide with many of the features of addictions. See if you can tell the similarities between idolatry and addictions in the passages below!

1. shame, fear, hunger Isa. 44:9-10
2. a deceived heart has turned him aside v.20
3. cannot see that he is holding fast to a lie v.20
4. walked after their own vanity Jer. 2:5
5. after things that do not profit 2:8
6. My fear is not in thee 2:19
7. forgot the Lord days without number 2:32
8. covered with confusion 3:25
9. destruction upon destruction 4:20
10. they have no understanding v.22
11. refuse to receive correction 5:3
12. they made their faces harder than a rock v.3
13. did not tremble at God's presence v.22

14. they had no delight in the word of the Lord 6:10
15. after other gods to their harm 7:6
16. they hold fast to deceit 8:5
17. no peace, no health, trouble v.15
18. they proceed from evil to evil 9:3
19. they are not valiant for the truth v.3
20. weary themselves to commit iniquity v.5

In my studies on idolatry, I have found that the phrases of this nature could conservatively be stretched to six to eight hundred phrases that refer to the expressions of idolatry.

Cleansing and healing (part 1)

Why will you still be struck down?
Why will you continue to rebel?
The whole head is sick,
and the whole heart faint.
From the sole of the foot even to the head,
there is no soundness in it,
but bruises and sores
and raw wounds;
they are not pressed out or bound up
or softened with oil.

Cause of Addictions

While I do not believe in the "disease concept" of addictions as it is presented by many, I readily admit that the Scriptures sometimes refer to our spiritual condition as an illness. Just as we experience physical birth, we may experience a spiritual birth. Just as we grow physically, we may grow spiritually. So, just as we may be physically ill, we can be spiritually ill (provided we have spiritual life found in Christ, to begin with.) And while the concerns of the day seem to be aimed toward healing, cleansing seems to no longer be an issue.

I can remember the time when people would pray for cleansing—now they pray for healing. Does that mean that we are clean now? Before speaking of Israel's condition as an illness in chapter 1:5-6, Isaiah pronounces their sin (Isaiah 1:4). The illness that Israel was experiencing was the result of their sin and rebellion. We don't need to be healed from sin; we need to be cleansed from sin.

> *Ah, sinful nation,*
>   *a people laden with iniquity,*
> *offspring of evildoers,*
>   *children who deal corruptly!*
> *They have forsaken the Lord,*
>   *they have despised the Holy One*

of Israel,
  they are utterly estranged.
Isaiah 1:4 ESV

Unfortunately, there is a lot of confusion today concerning spiritual cleansing. While doing a search on "Google" for a picture to fit my writing, I discovered all kinds of invitations for addressing spiritual issues that were inadequately unrelated. When dealing with spiritual issues we must be certain that our methods are prescribed by God. Many of the methods I discovered are man-made (not of God.) How can I say that with such assurance? Simply because many of the presentations that I discovered had nothing to do with Jesus. Can you name anyone who was more spiritual than Jesus? Jesus lived a life that was completely spiritual. The words of Jesus were spiritual. Most importantly, the blood that Jesus shed is the only source provided by God for spiritual cleansing. Pray for cleansing! Seek out cleansing! Cleansing comes before healing

Cleansing and healing (part 2)

You blind Pharisee! First clean the inside of the cup and the plate, that the outside also may be clean. **Matthew 23:26 ESV**

Cleanliness has a direct effect on our health. It is a known fact that physical impurities can be harmful. In an article titled, "The Dangers of a Dirty House", Wise Projects makes the following statement:

> "Most people have experienced, or at least aware, of the inconveniences caused by an untidy, unclean home. Plus, a tidy house is generally much nicer to live in. But were you aware that a dirty house could actually lead to a multitude of health problems too?"

The old-timers used to refer to "sin-sick souls". I guess we have outgrown that kind vernacular! To seek healing from God without cleansing is hypocrisy. One of the definitions for an addiction is a desire, a lust, or a passion. Peter reveals to us how our ungodly desires can damage our souls. (The NIV uses the word "desires", KJV "lust", ESV "passions") Just as physical impurities can cause damage to our bodies, spiritual impurities can cause damage to our souls.

> *Dear friends, I urge you, as foreigners and exiles, to abstain from sinful desires, which wage war against your soul.* **1 Peter 2:11, NIV**

Do you allow things into your house that would cause you to be sick? Not if you are in your right mind! Do you think that it is God's will for you to allow things into your house that would make you sick? No, no more than it is God's will for us to allow something to stay in our lives that causes harm to our souls! More than anything, God wants us to be at our best spiritually. As the old saying goes, "God loves us just as we are, but He loves us too much to let us stay as we are!"

I realize the concerns that some have for the pain that many have suffered either leading to addiction or after choosing an addiction. And, while I realize the importance of healing when it comes to addictions, I believe that the bigger issue is cleansing. As with physical dirt, an unclean soul causes the inconvenience of impairing our vision. An unclean soul cannot see things as God does. Though rarely mentioned, reverencing God is a major issue for confronting addictions. One of the central ingredients of reverencing God is the sense of awe there is of God. Awe in made of vision.

Where is no vision, the people
perish.
Proverbs 29:18

Cleansing and healing (part 3)

Purge me with hyssop, and I shall be clean;
  wash me, and I be whiter than snow.
Let me hear joy and shall gladness;
  let the bones that You have broken rejoice.
Hide Your face from my sins,
  and blot out all my iniquities.
Create in me a clean heart, O God,
  and renew a right spirit within me.
Psalms 51:7-10 ESV

In Psalms 51, David asked for cleansing before asking for healing. Healing is not always guaranteed; cleansing is.1 John 1:9 tells us that "if we confess our sins, He is faithful and just to forgive us our sins, and to cleanse us from all unrighteousness." A broken heart is a clean heart. You will never escape the physical impurities of the world that cause sicknesses that destroy your body. You can escape the spiritual impurities of the world that will destroy your soul.

An ailment can be called a dysfunction. We were made to trust in God. That is how we were designed to function. The deadliest spiritual ailment that we face is unbelief. Unbelief can lead to addictions because addictions are nothing more than a form of idolatry. Rather than trusting in the true and living God, we sometimes turn to false gods. Ridding ourselves of idols requires cleansing.

Think of how much we are all like the little boy who was told not to get his good clothes dirty. In addition, since he did not know how to play without getting dirty, he was not allowed outside without supervision. Well, the boy snuck outside the house, got his clothes dirty, and suffered a terrible scrap. Do you think that the boy went farther from home after suffering an injury? No, he decided to go back inside the house no matter how disappointed his parents may become. We all know the story of when a parent sees a child in such a situation. "Let me get you out of those dirty clothes", is the first thing the parent says. The next thing is to clean the wound. Do you think that the wound will heal if it is not first cleansed?

In Christ, we are given a set of clean clothes just like the little boy. We don't know how to live any more than the boy knows how to play, without the supervision of the Holy Spirit. God has allowed us safety so long as we "dwell in the secret place of the Most High." But, outside the shelter and supervision of His Eminence, we get hurt and dirty. Unfortunately, some of us don't go back to the safety of "home" as the little boy did. But, whenever we return to God, just like the loving parents of the little boy, God makes sure we are clean. One of the added bonuses only available to those who are in Christ is the joy that David speaks about which is the joy that Peter described as inexpressible. (1 Peter 1:8) Better than playing in the mud!

I, being of a sound mind (part 1)

> *God may perhaps grant them repentance leading to a knowledge of the truth, and they may come to their senses and escape from the snare of the devil, after being captured by him to do his will.*
> *2 Timothy 2:25b-26 ESV*

As far back as my childhood, I remember the phrase- "I being of a sound mind" used in the last will and testament of individuals. After nearly fifty-eight years upon this earth, and eight years of sobriety, the meaning behind those words become more significant. Coming to one's senses is another way of stating that one is of a sound mind. But it is impossible to be of a sound mind without being on one accord with God. **Outside of God, there is no sanity.** Addictions are just one expression of insanity.

The biggest question that confronts us concerning addictions is whether I am able to face God. If this is not settled at the beginning of our quest for sobriety, we will have a weak foundation. If we do not begin our sobriety on one accord with God, we don't have the safety that is found in escaping Hell. This should be the "first order of business" for us who have given ourselves to things that are not of God (such as addictions.) The ultimate remedy of addictions is to choose God over everything else. We come to our senses as we choose what is of the greatest value. Can you name anything of greater value than being on one accord with God? John Bunyan's pastor, John Gifford has a word on this in the preface to *Pilgrim's Progress*.

> "Consider what an ill bargain thou wilt make, to sell thy precious soul for short continuance in thy sins and pleasures. If that man drives but an ill trade, who, to gain the world, should lose his soul (Matt 16:26), then, certainly, thou art far worse that sells thy soul for a very trifle. O it is pity that so precious a thing should be parted withal, to be made a prey for the devouring lion, for that which is worse than nothing! … The wise merchant that sought a goodly pearl, having found one, sold all that he had, not himself, not his soul, and all that he sold was in itself not worth a farthing, and yet obtained the pearl (Matt 13:45,46). Paul made the

like exchange when he threw away
his own righteousness, which was
but rags, yea, filthy rags (Isa 64:6),
and put on the garment of
salvation, and cast away to the
dunghill that which was once his
gain, and won Christ (Phil 3:8).
Thou needest not cast away thy
soul for puddle pleasures; behold
the fountain of living water is set
open, and thou invited to it, to take
and drink thy belly, thy soul full,
without price or money (Isa 55:2)."

I, being of a sound mind (part 2)

*God may perhaps grant them
repentance leading to a knowledge of the
truth, and they may come to their senses
and escape from the snare of the devil, after
being captured by him to do his will.*
2 Timothy 2:25b-26 ESV

Have you ever met a person who had "taken
leave of their senses?" Have you ever been
such a person? Through the years, I have
"taken leave of my senses" in various degrees.
This is rightly defined by some as "being out of

touch with reality." Although it may appear to be blissful, "taking leave of your senses" is a woeful and agonizing state. Insanity distorts the truth. When someone is insane, they cannot be reasoned with. Insane people do not know what is real. I cannot tell you how many times God would tell me not to be as the horse or the mule, which have no understanding (Psalms 32:9) regarding addictions."

We are not able to function without our senses. Perhaps, you have seen people that are so out of touch with reality that they are not be able to provide themselves with the necessities of life. This is often noticed among those who are diagnosed with various mental issues. If someone does not lend a hand, these people will have no life. But there is a spiritual aspect to being out of touch with reality that is directly related to addiction.

For the people that Paul was speaking of in 2 Timothy to come to their senses, they would need repentance leading to a knowledge of the truth. Repentance is needed for those of us who have accepted the lies concerning addictions. And while it is true that many seek repentance (change), they want to do so by the same distorted senses that are out of touch with the Spirit of Truth who communicates through the Word of God.

While there are those who are so out of touch with reality that they are not able to provide themselves with bodily necessities, there are also those of us who lack spiritual necessities. Just as there is no life for those who lack physical necessities, there is no life for those who lack spiritual necessities. It is no wonder why God said that man shall not live by bread alone, but by every word that proceeds out of the mouth of God (Deuteronomy 8:3).

The mistaken identity

> *As they were gathering in Galilee, Jesus said to them, "The Son of Man is about to be delivered into the hands of men, and they will kill Him, and He will be raised on the third day." And they were greatly distressed.* **Matthew 17:22-23 ESV**

While growing up, I enjoyed the company of twin uncles. One of the twins lived in my hometown for a time, while the other only would visit occasionally. One day while the uncle from out of town was visiting, he told us a funny story. As he had decided to pay a visit to the neighborhood bar, he met a female acquaintance of his twin. Since his twin had moved away, it had been some time since anyone in Cleveland had seen him. My uncle said that the woman said that she was glad to see him and that it had been a long time. When the woman asked for a hug, my uncle said, "Lady, I'm not who you think that I am!"

My uncle's situation was harmless. But, if we are not able to recognize how Jesus is able to eradicate the addictions that haunt us, the effect can be devastating. Unfortunately, Jesus' disciples did not recognize the mission that Jesus was sent to fulfill during his time on earth. This should come as no surprise since it was already foretold by the prophet Isaiah that no one would believe that the Messiah would be sent to pay for our sins:

> *Who has believed what he has heard from us? And to whom has the arm of the Lord been revealed?*
> **Isaiah 53:1 ESV**

Jesus could join my uncle stating, "I'm not Who you think I am!" Jesus is much greater than we can ever imagine. Romans chapter 5 tells us so.

> *For while we were still weak, at the right time Christ died for the ungodly. For one will scarcely die for*

> *a righteous person—though perhaps*
> *for a good person one would dare*
> *even to die— but God shows His*
> *love for us in that while we were*
> *still sinners, Christ died for us.*
> *Romans 5:6-8 ESV*

There is no forgiveness of sin outside of Christ. I dare anyone to tell me how to be forgiven outside of the blood of Christ. There is no religion that was ever invented to makes a provision for forgiveness. The best that they can do is to tell you to start where you are, through your own power and become a good person (not godly but good.) This is the problem with whatever program excludes Christ. First, they treat Christ as though His death were in vain. Second, they act as though people can become right with God apart from Christ. Go to a traditional group for addictions and you will never hear a word about sin. Yet, sin is the biggest problem we have (it is the source of all our problems.)

Are you an addict? (part 1)

You study the Scriptures diligently because you think that in them you have eternal life. These are the very Scriptures that testify about Me.
John 5:39 ESV

You pore over the Scriptures because you presume that by them you possess eternal life. These are the very words that testify about Me. **Berean Study Bible**

You diligently search the Scriptures because you think to have eternal life in them, and these are they bearing witness concerning Me. **Berean Literal Bible**

Alcoholics Anonymous is correct in stating that alcoholism is cunning, baffling and powerful. But then, Psalm 19:7b says that "the testimony of the Lord is sure, making wise the simple." For years, I was confused concerning what is erroneously known as "the disease concept." It took years of discernment while being exposed to the Word of God, the impressions that the Spirit of God has made, guidance through others and personal experience before I became totally convinced that addiction is not a disease. And just for the record, the *Alcoholics Anonymous book never*

said that alcoholism is a disease. It went as far as to say that it is like a disease. I, also, agree with part of Narcotics Anonymous' definition of an addict. (I would stop where it is stated that addiction is an illness.)

> Most of us do not have to think twice about this question. We know! Our whole life and thinking was centered in drugs in one form or another – the getting and using and finding ways and means to get more. We lived to use and used to live. Very simply, an addict is a man or woman whose life is controlled by drugs. We are people in the grip of a continuing and progressive illness whose ends are always the same: jails, institutions and death. - Who is an Addict?

We are all born with a love for sin. We are tempted by sin in many ways. Who would argue that addictions are not tempting? Are diseases something that tempt us? Allow me the liberty of using Narcotics Anonymous' definition of an addict to describe a sinner!

> Who is a sinner? Most of us do not have to twice about this question. We know! Our whole life and

> thinking were centered on sin in one form or another.- the thoughts, the attitudes and the actions aimed towards sinning more and more. We lived to sin and sinned to live. Very simply. A sinner is a man or woman whose life is controlled by sin.

It can be said that we are all addicted to sin. If this is the case then we are all addicts. Yet, one thing that we must consider is the evidence of addiction in someone's life. If the person no longer engages in addiction, are they still an addict? While, the disease concept says yes, I would beg to differ.

As a writer, I am committed to writing on a regular basis (usually daily.) It is as much of a practice as an addiction. One of the authors in my library makes the point that while a disease is not something that we practice, addictions are something that we practice. If I did not write for a whole year, could I still call myself a writer?

It is very unfortunate that the masses have been confused about this issue. I see it as a direct result of people forsaking and rejecting the Word of God to define life. Addictions are a part of life and if we do not look to the Author of life for answers, by the Spirit of Truth, we are looking for answers from the father of lies.

Are you an addiction? (part 2)

> *So to keep me from becoming conceited because of the surpassing greatness of the revelations, a thorn was given me in the flesh, a messenger of Satan to harass me, to keep me from becoming conceited.*
> **2 Corinthians 12:7 ESV**

I don't think that anyone likes being wrong! Correct me if I am wrong (no pun intended!) I remember talking with my youngest uncle for about two hours on the validity of Christ. After all his excuses for rejecting Christ, his final words were, "There's nothing wrong with being wrong!" On the contrary, being wrong can be costly (I won't go into detail.)

Arthur Fonzarelli, better known as "'Fonzie'" or "'The Fonz'", was played by Henry Winkler for the full 11 year run of the show *Happy Days*. Fonzie thinks he is never wrong and, consequently, has trouble admitting so. He attempts to say he was wrong in the episode titled "Tell it to the Marines," which originally aired on December 16, 1975, but can only get as far as an r with an unidentifiable vowel. He also has trouble apologizing, saying the word, "sorry", as evidenced in the episode titled "My Fair Fonzie," which originally aired on November 22, 1977.

Years ago, I heard a friend who suggested that the thorn in the flesh that Paul was referring to may have been an addiction. One of the problems with my friend's theory is that Paul was speaking of something that was physical, while addictions begin on a spiritual level (as we exhibit worship towards an addiction over God.) Like many others, my friend was duped into believing addictions to be a disease! Such erroneous thinking has cost us! Many a soul has gone to hell because they never owned up to the sinfulness of addictions and the need for God's forgiveness. And multitudes lie in confusion concerning the matter. We turn our attention toward healing rather than deep doses of repentance.

It has been said that we are our own worst enemies. A long time ago, I discovered this to be true as I considered how we overrated ourselves. Many of us consider ourselves to be so good that we don't need repentance, we need healing. I believe that there are, many who do not have a deep understanding of sin. To intensify my sobriety, I was once led to purchase and read Puritan writing called *The Sinfulness of Sin*. I am greatly encouraged over a new Facebook friend who has dedicated his time and energy to sharing many of A.W. Pink's writings. Here something that Pink wrote on sin.

"Those who are inwardly taught of God discover there is abundantly more of evil in their defiled natures and sinful actions than ever they realized before. There is as great and real a difference between that general notion which the natural man has of sin and that experiential and intuitional knowledge of it which is possessed by the Divinely quickened soul as there is between the mere picture of a lion and being confronted by a living lion as it meets us roaring in the way."

Are you an addict? (part 3)

Then came the disciples to Jesus apart, and said, Why could not we cast him out? And Jesus said unto them, Because of your unbelief: for verily I say unto you, If ye have faith as a grain of mustard seed, ye shall say unto this mountain, Remove hence to yonder place; and it shall remove; and nothing shall be impossible unto you. Howbeit this kind goeth not out but by prayer and fasting.
Matthew 17:19-21 KJV

I once had the privilege of being incarcerated for sixty days while my attention was totally aimed towards Christ. It was a blessing to be able to see things clearly during that time and to minister to other inmates. My incarceration was initiated by a warrant that had been issued years before. I decided to turn myself in so that I could benefit from some of the benefits that the V.A. would not render so long as I had a warrant.

While jailhouse food can be called a "forced fast", I also fasted voluntarily in my worship towards God. I started playing with my cellmates over the food advertisements from whatever reading we could acquire. I would playfully moan and groan over the food advertisements as though lusting after sex. What I was stating was something that we learn very early in fasting. Fasting teaches discernment. Through fasting, you learn very early whether you are hungry because you have a <u>lust</u> for food or if you are hungry because you have a <u>need</u> for food. Through fasting, you can learn to discern what is physical from what is spiritual.

I do not believe that anyone is born addicted to anything but sin (except for children who are exposed to drugs in the womb.) And we will all be sinners until the day we die (if the Lord does not return first.) We make the choice of becoming an addict to various substances and/or activities. We are, also, free to make the choice of relinquishing our addiction through the power of God. And so, we do not have to remain addicts for the rest of our lives.

Not until recently, have people began to address the true spiritual aspects of addictions for the idols that they are. I know this for a fact because, in all my years of fighting an addiction to crack, I did not find anything of this nature until the early 2000s. (That was after my initial unpublished work in the mid-90s) Perhaps, we really didn't want the answers that God has had for us all along. Many still do not want those answers!

To label addictions as idolatry is based on the discernment that is found in the Word of God. To yield ourselves completely to God gives us discernment. Fasting is a means of yielding ourselves completely to God. In God there is truth. Here's an easy question for you! If something is not true, then what is it? If we are not bond and connected to the Author of Truth, we associate ourselves with the Father of lies (the Devil) by default. Most people do not do so intentionally. I have this saying about con artists:

Have you ever met someone who set out to con you and told you beforehand? Hey, come here and let me trick you out of all your money. How would you respond? Satan is clever enough to make you

think that he is your best friend and
that he has the right idea about
everything.

I have been blessed to avoid taking the word
of others in matters that drastically affect my
life. That's why I would always look for other
solutions to addictions whenever I had the
privilege of receiving treatment from the V.A.
instead of fully embracing their philosophy on
addictions. Far too often, people listen to others
not knowing if their allegiance is given to the
Author of Truth.

Please believe me! I have studied the
"disease concept" of addictions to the point of
reading textbooks. It is a shame that even Bible
colleges and seminaries concentrate so much
on the physiological implications of addictions.
One thing that I love about biblical fasting is
that it separates physical from spiritual like no
other practice. Here is where you find clarity!
Here is where you find God! And where you
find God, you find power and truth!

Captivated

*Call unto me, and I will answer thee, and show thee great and mighty things, which thou knowest not. **Jeremiah 33:3 KJV***

*Call to me and I will answer you, and will tell you great and hidden things that you have not known. **ESV***

Once upon a time, I was as mesmerized with drugs as the idols worshippers that opposed Elijah.

> *And they took the bull that was given them, and they prepared it and called upon the name of Baal from morning until noon, saying, "O Baal, answer us!" But there was no voice, and no one answered. And they limped around the altar that they had made. ... And they cried aloud and cut themselves after their custom with swords and lances, until the blood gushed out upon them. And as midday passed, they raved on until the time of the offering of the oblation, but there was no voice. No one answered; no*

one paid attention. **1 Kings 18:26, 28-29 ESV**

What I found was that I did not have all the answers and the answers that I was looking for were not found in addiction. The answers that addictions gave were the same as the answers that God told Israel that they would find in chasing after idols as well as what the "wine bibber" is promised.

> *The Lord will send on you curses, confusion, and frustration in all that you undertake to do, until you are destroyed and perish quickly on account of the evil of your deeds, because you have forsaken Me. ... so that you are driven mad by the sights that your eyes see.*
> **Deuteronomy 28:20, 34 ESV**
>
> *so that you are driven mad by the sights that your eyes see.*
> **Proverbs 23:33 Contemporary English Version**
>
> *Your sufferings will make you lose your mind.*
> **Proverbs 23:33 Good News Translation**

One of the things that I asked God for, as He gave me the strength and the wisdom to overcome my drug addiction through the matchless power of Christ, was excitement. My prayer went something like this: "Lord God, You know that I find a lot of excitement in my drug use, and yet I desire to love You with all my heart. And so, dear God, would you please take that excitement from me or replace it with another excitement."

Time after time, God has honored my prayer by sometimes giving me more excitement than I can handle as we labor together. One of the greater compliments that my wife has ever paid is when she told me that I was the most exciting man that she had ever met. I attribute this to how God keeps His promise that if we call on Him, He would answer us and show us great and mighty things. Things that conquer addictions. Things that make us whole...

Integrity battles discontentment

And he said, "Naked I came from my mother's womb, and naked shall I return. The Lord gave, and the Lord has taken away; blessed be the name of the Lord." In all this Job did not sin or charge God with wrong.
... And the Lord said to Satan, "Have you

> considered my servant Job, that there is
> none like him on the earth, a blameless and
> upright man, who fears God and turns
> away from evil? He still holds fast his
> integrity, although you incited me against
> him to destroy him without reason." ... Then
> his wife said to him, "Do you still hold fast
> your integrity? Curse God and die." But he
> said to her, "You speak as one of the foolish
> women would speak. Shall we receive good
> from God, and shall we not receive evil?"
> In all this Job did not sin with his lips.
> **Job 1:21-22, 2:3, 9-10 ESV**

Discontentment lies at the heart and soul of every addiction in one form or another. Discontentment has the potential of producing ungodly attitudes and actions. To say that Job was discontent with his situation would be an understatement. But, how did Job respond to his discontentment? Did he take up a crack pipe as I once did in my discontentment? Did Job look to another god or a distortion of the true and living God?

Job's wife told him to curse God. Does not sin (especially idolatrous addictions) accuse God of being unreasonable? Instead, Job blessed the name of the Lord. To bless means to speak well of. This is the effect of a reverential disposition. It is the measurement of our reverence for God that gives us vision.

Cause of Addictions

Who would argue that we need vision to break the "spell" of addiction?

Effect

False repentance
The fear factor
Our daily walk
The presence of the Lord
Express yourself
Destiny
To whom be glory
Beyond understanding
Magnitude and intensity
Check your motives
Handwriting on the wall
Maturity
Full or empty
Be not silent 1 & 2
Rest 1 & 2
High definition
Your honor
The outer limits
Hold it right there
Delight in the Lord
Reserved/preserved
National security
Promotion vs. demotion
Trained

The effect of an addiction is the absorption of our attention. Addictions, also, devour our time, resources, relationships… our lives. They cause us to be unstable and unfruitful in many areas. Addictions cause us to be less human and are a threat to society.

False Repentance

The teachers of the law and the chief priests looked for a way to arrest Him immediately, because they knew He had spoken this parable against them. But they were afraid of the people. **Luke 20:19**

As I read this passage, I think back on all the times that I would have just as well continued indulging in an ungodly, idolatrous addiction were it not for the grace of God. Today's passage says that the only reason that the chief priests did not arrest Jesus immediately is that they were afraid of the people. They were just waiting and watching for an opportunity to do as they pleased.

That's just the way it is when we are not motivated to leave an addiction out of our commitment to the Lord. We reserve the right to do as we please so long as it pleases us. Whether it is pleasing to God is hardly the issue**. I would not even call this sobriety.** Some might refer to it as a "dry drunk."

This is what is commonly known as being under the influence. The interesting thing about being under the influence is that there is no time limit. Case in point- people sit in prison for years, decades, while remaining abstinent, but still under the influence of an addiction.

Upon being released from prison, they go straight to the object of their addiction.

Just as the chief priests, we take the risk of leaning on our own understanding. The thing that is necessary is for us to acknowledge that God's thoughts are not our thoughts, and His ways are not our ways, to begin the process of repentance and be on one accord with Him. *Repentance- some may refer to recovery, restoration, deliverance...

The Fear Factor

It is a fearful thing to fall into the hands of the living God. Hebrews 10:31

Here is a sobering thought (perhaps the most sobering in all the universe.) It is the summation of what occurs upon the systematic rejection of Christ (read verses 28 and 29.) Many do not realize what an insult it is toward God to reject His Son. This is true when it comes to dealing with addictions as well.

To say that one has a spiritual program and yet exclude Christ is a lie.

Here are the very words of Jesus;

> *It is the Spirit who gives life; the flesh profits nothing. The words that I speak to you are spirit, and they are life.* **John 6:63**

Why is it that excluding Christ from a program for addictions such an insult to God? I can think of a multitude of reasons. Here are what may be the top two:

> 1. Without Christ, there is no forgiveness from God (therefore there is no true union either.)
> 2. Without Christ, there is no sure guidance.

Don't get me wrong! Reverence for God also refers to our love, honor, respect, and awe, but we cannot disregard the fear factor behind reverence as well! God is not to be trifled with!

Our Daily Walk

> *Blessed are those who listen to me, watching daily at my doors,*

waiting at my doorway.
Proverbs 8:34

Here is a reminder that **our walk is daily**.

A walk is comprised of steps. Those steps start to add, and we are headed in a definite direction.

Some say that we are either moving closer to God, or we are moving away from Him. One thing that I can tell you for sure is that whether you listen to the voice of wisdom (coming from God) or the voice of folly (coming from addictions), **your walk will lead you into places you never imagined**!

The Presence of the Lord

For how then will it be known that Your people and I have found grace in Your sight, except You go with us? **Exodus 33:16**

The presence of the Lord bears great significance in all we do. One thing that we can be sure of is that God does not dwell where there is evil. In our deepest hours of temptation and failure, God is there. Yet and still, there is a difference between temptation and actual sin. There is a difference between premeditated, willful sin and "ignorant" sin.

But, to know that you have found grace in the sight of the Lord makes all the difference in the world. It all goes back to trusting Christ as our righteousness before God. Jesus has promised all those who trust Him that He would never leave us or forsake us.

One of the problems with addictions is that we forsake the things that really matter. **I am humbled by the fact that God often continues to protect those who have no concern about His presence while seeking an addiction**. I did this myself. It is amazing that He allowed me to live during my times of presumption.

This was a serious situation for Moses and the children of Israel. Perhaps, even more serious than our addictions. Both are life or death situations (to be sure.) Moses and the children of Israel could plainly see that they were in a life or death situation.

One of the problems with an addiction is that we cannot always see it as a life or death situation.

But the scriptures are very plain about this. The wages of sin is death (Romans 6:23). **I guess that is why Satan has the world to claim addictions as a disease. For if**

**addictions are a disease, then people don't
need to turn to Jesus for forgiveness.**

Express Yourself

*In the same way, faith by itself, if it is not
accompanied by action, is dead.* **James 2:17**

Most of us are capable of expressing ourselves
verbally. Almost everyone is capable of
expressing themselves non-verbally. James
2:14-26 mainly refers to non-verbal
communication. Three of the methods of
communicating that we have chosen God over
addictions is through our abstinence, fasting,
and communing with God. Chapter 6 of
Turning to God from Idols refer to these as
"Acts of Repentance."

Our communion with God is where the
change begins. It is as God speaks to us that we
are able to see Him for the magnificent God
that He is (and the unworthiness of addictions.)
Our communion with God can, also, be
referred to as a conversation. The conversation
is made of three parts.

James 2:14-26 concerns this third part of our
conversation.

1. Listening to God.
2. Talking to God.
3. Doing what God says.

"When we do what God says we are communing with God in an intimate manner as well. When we do what God says with the right attitude, we agree with Him.

I like the way that this is expressed in the KJV with the use of the word 'conversation' in various passages which is presented as 'life, live, etc'" in other versions.

What we see is yet another method of communication between us and God. As we do what God says with the right kind of attitude, it is a practice of worship (as we are telling God that He is worthy of our obedience.) This is what others 'hear' as well. And when we don't do as He says, or do it with a bad attitude, we are telling Him, as well as others, that He is not worthy."
- *Turning to God from Idols,* Madison

Here are some of the passages (negative and positive):

Among whom also we all had our conversation in times past in the lusts of our flesh, **Ephesians 2:3**

And delivered just Lot, vexed with the filthy conversation of the wicked. **2 Peter 2:7**

Only let your conversation be as it becometh the gospel of Christ. **Philippians 1:27a**

But as He which hath called you is holy, so be ye holy in all manner of conversation. **1 Peter 1:15**

Your conversation with God could be the most sensational conversation ever.

Destiny

I have been with you for twenty years now. Your sheep and goats have not miscarried, nor have I eaten rams from your flocks. I did not bring you animals torn by wild beasts; I bore the loss myself. And you demanded payment from me for whatever was stolen by day or night. This was my situation: The heat consumed me in the daytime and the cold at night, and sleep fled from my eyes. It was like this for the twenty years I was in your household. I worked for you fourteen years for your two daughters and six years for your flocks, and you changed my wages ten times. If the God of my father, the God of Abraham and the Fear of Isaac, had not been with me, you would surely have sent me away empty-handed. But God has seen my hardship and the toil of my hands, and last night He rebuked you." **Genesis 31:42**

Here is an account of Jacob's dealing with his father-in-law (Laban.) Just like Jacob worked for Laban for twenty years, I worked for addiction for twenty years.

My addiction was even more cunning and treacherous than Laban. It is important that we realize the treachery of addiction! It is of greater importance that we realize the faithfulness and the presence of God in each situation as Jacob did as well.

A good reading on this is "The Practice of the Presence of God" by Brother Lawrence. Here is an excerpt;

"That we need only to recognize GOD intimately present with us, to address ourselves to Him every moment, that we may beg His assistance for knowing His will in things doubtful, and for rightly performing those which we plainly see He requires of us, offering them to Him before we do them, and giving Him thanks when we have done."

To Whom be Glory

Grace and peace to you from God our Father and the Lord Jesus Christ, who gave himself for our sins to rescue us from the present evil age, according to the will of our God and Father, to Whom be glory for ever and ever. Amen. **Galatians 1:4**

I remember going through drug treatment while working at the Post Office and upon discharge, after collecting my paycheck, I went on a shopping spree. Man, I felt great! I thought that I really had it together. All the while, I was not seeking the Lord in my abstinence. I can remember how I sought to find peace, satisfaction, and joy in the things that I had purchased only to discover that they would no more give me what I was seeking than the drugs that I had forsaken. Call it what you may, but I had rejected the Lord as King over my life. This is the evil that God rescues us from.

> "My people have committed two sins:
> They have forsaken me,
> the spring of living water,
> and have dug their own cisterns,
> broken cisterns that cannot hold water.
> **Jeremiah 2:13**

The evil rejection of Christ may take on various forms. It may not even appear to be evil by the world's standards. But I can tell you by experience that anything devoid of Christ is not of God and therefore evil.

I was surprised to learn that the phrase "anti-Christ" in the original language has such a subtle meaning. The Greek word for "anti" in this instance means "instead of." One of the emphases of *Turning to God from Idols* is how addictions are first and foremost an offense to the Almighty. How could we ever get around this? Why would we want to? Jesus is not only worthy of the attention that I gave to myself and my shopping; Jesus, also, is able to provide the things that we could never get from ourselves, this world, or anywhere else. But, first and foremost, Jesus gives glory to God!

Beyond Understanding (Part 1)

Not unto us, O Lord, not unto us, but unto Thy name give glory, for Thy mercy, and for Thy truth's sake. Wherefore should the heathen say, Where is now their God? But our God is in the heavens: He hath done whatsoever He hath pleased. Their idols are silver and gold, the work of men's hands. They have mouths, but they speak not: eyes have they, but they see not: They have ears, but they hear not: noses have they, but they smell not: They have hands, but they handle not: feet have they, but they walk not: neither speak they through their throat. They that make them are like unto them; so is every one that trusteth in them. O Israel, trust thou in the Lord: He is their help and their shield. Psalms 115:1-9 KJV

Addictions go beyond our understanding without the truth of God unmasking their deception.

The issue of addiction can be very complicating. The reason behind this is because you are dealing with something that is foreign. The element of addiction is an instrument of the devil. Dealing with an addiction can difficult because the devil is a liar and a deceiver (Turning to God from Idols, back cover.) Gaining understanding from God is essential to our sobriety.

Cool Hand Luke is a 1967 American prison drama film directed by Stuart Rosenberg, starring Paul Newman and featuring George Kennedy in an Oscar-winning performance. Newman stars in the title role as Luke, a prisoner in a Florida prison camp who refuses to submit to the system. The most famous line in the movie is where the warden says to Luke, "What we have here is failure to communicate."

Well, that's the problem with us and God whenever we decide to chase after idolatrous addictions. That is why **I propose that the first phase of dealing with an addiction is reasoning**. This was God's plea to Israel (come let us reason together). As quiet as it is kept, this is not only true in my presentation (turning to God from idols), it is the very same in any and every system, program, method... of dealing with addictions. The problem is that we have no understanding outside of Christ.

*The natural person does not accept
the things of the Spirit of God, for
they are folly to Him, and He is not
able to understand them because
they are spiritually discerned.*
1 Corinthians 2:14 ESV

The fact of the matter is that **we must be born again to be able to communicate with God**. We must be spiritually born or we are just as lifeless as the idols that we bow to. In fact, apart from Christ, we have no interest in the true and living God (though some pretend they do.)

*as it is written: "None is righteous,
no, not one; no one understands;
no one seeks for God.
All have turned aside;
together they have become worthless;
no one does good, not even one."
"There is no fear of God before their eyes."*
Romans 2:10-12, 18

Magnitude and Intensity

*And we all, with unveiled face, beholding
the glory of the Lord, are being transformed
into the same image from one degree of glory
to another. For this comes from the Lord
who is the Spirit.*
2 Corinthians 3:18

The Lord Jesus Christ was fully used of God in the most mighty of fashions, crescendo in His greatest service to God and man by bridging the gap between God and man in dying for our sins.

Now, while we cannot die for someone else's sins, God wants to use us just the same. Many argue that God can use anyone. True enough. The question is whether you will be used by God voluntarily or involuntarily. Perhaps the greatest evidence that someone has abandoned the self-pleasing life of addiction is their longing to be used of God.

Just as there are degrees of reverence for God, there are degrees in which we agree to be used of God. There are, also, degrees or levels of sobriety.

The magnitude and intensity to which are (voluntarily) used of God depend on how much we reverence Him. The opportunities and abilities that we have as individuals may vary.

The question is whether we are growing more into the image of Christ. This is what true sobriety looks like. Much of what people call sobriety or "recovery" today is just as self-serving as other addictions.

One of the things that bothered me greatly during my self-indulging life of drugs and illicit sex was the thought that one day everybody would be at my gravesite stating, "He wasn't about nothing. He didn't do anything worthwhile. **He was of no help to anyone** ..." All along I knew that God desires better. If God is not all that great to us then it is only natural that we will not desire to be used by Him greatly.

This is, ironically, true of the gods of addictions as well. The greater the value that we place on an addiction the more we are used by it with magnitude and intensity. Only the true and living God desires our all. Jesus gives us the ability to be all that God wants so that we can do all that God wants for His glory and His alone of which He is worthy!

Check Your Motives

> *Do not love the world or the things in the world. If anyone loves the world, the love of the Father is not in him. For all that is in the world—the desires of the flesh and the desires of the eyes and pride of life—is not from the Father but is from the world. And the world is passing away along with its desires, but whoever does the will of God abides forever.* **1 John 2:15-17**

What is your main reason abstaining from an addiction? Is it because it ruins your life? Or was it because you recognize it as being wrong in the sight of God? Are you more concerned about the way addiction affects your relationships, your job, your health or the way it affects God?

I am not saying that we should not be concerned about other areas, but if we do not abstain out of reverence for God, then our motives will be less than pure.

It's really a question of what we value. Do we value God or do we value family, possessions or reputation more? Jesus Christ explained to His followers that there is a decision they all had to make. In Matthew 10: 37-39 He said, "He who loves father or mother more than Me is not worthy of Me. And he who loves son or daughter more than Me is not worthy of me. And he who does not take his cross and follow after Me is not worthy of Me. He who finds his life will lose it, and he who loses his life for My sake will find it."

In a related verse, Jesus said, "If any man will come after me, let him deny himself, and take up his cross daily, and follow me." (Luke 9:23) In a most worthy reading called *Hard to Believe*, John MacArthur states that the original Greek word for "deny" means "to refuse to associate with".

> "The thought is that if you want to be Christ's disciple, and receive forgiveness and eternal life, you must refuse to associate any longer with the person you are! You are sick of your sinful self and want nothing to do with you anymore."
> -   MacArthur

> *"I the Lord search the heart*
> *and test the mind,*
> *to give every man according to his ways,*
> *according to the fruit of his deeds."*
> *Jeremiah 17:10 ESV*

The title of *Turning to God from Idols* comes from
1 Thessalonians 1:9, which commended the Thessalonians for "turning to God from idols to serve the living and true God." In his article titled "Idols of the Heart", David Powlinson states

"*idolatry is far the most frequently discussed problem in the scriptures*"

Perhaps, this is because <u>the One who inspired the scriptures knew that idolatry would be an ever-increasing problem</u>.

I am, personally, convinced that if the Word of God had nothing to say about addictions, then God would not have created us.

"The purpose of this book is to uncover the true-identity of addictions, to encourage the reader to continually turn to Christ for answers, and to promote the joy of fellowshipping with the living and true God with others."
- *Turning to God from Idols,*
Gregory Madison

The Handwriting on the Wall

This is the interpretation of the matter: Mene, God has numbered the days of your kingdom and brought it to an end; Tekel, you have been weighed in the balances and found wanting; Peres, your kingdom is divided and given to the Medes and Persians." Daniel 5:26-28

Daniel may as well have been writing to the addicts of today. There are so many experiences that King Belshazzar lived that are like those of addicts.

> v.4 praised the gods
> v.6 Then the king's color changed,
> and his thoughts alarmed him;
> his limbs gave way,
> and his knees knocked together.
> v.9 King Belshazzar was greatly alarmed,
> and his color changed,
> and his lords were perplexed.
> v. 22 have not humbled your heart,
> v.23 you have lifted up yourself against
> the Lord of heaven
> And you have praised the gods of silver
> and gold, of bronze, iron, wood, and
> stone,
> which do not see or hear or know,
> but the God in whose hand is your breath,

and whose are all your ways, you have not
honored.
And of course, we see three other
similarities from
vv. 26-28

1. God has numbered the days of your
   kingdom and brought it to an end.
2. You have been weighed in the
balance
   and found wanting.
3. Your kingdom is divided and given
to the
   Medes and Persians

There are at least 3 things that apply to
addicts in this context.

1. Sooner or later addicts find that they
are
   not in control (unfortunately, some
don't
   find out until they die.)

2. Addictions are futile.

3. Loss is eminent with addictions.

Maturity

We all stumble in many ways. Anyone who is never at fault in what they say is perfect, able to keep their whole body in check.
James 3:2 NIV

The word "perfect" in this verse refers to maturity. Maturity is one of the best words that can be used to describe the process of breaking free of an addiction (turning to God from idols is an accurate definition as well.) James tells us that as we mature, we are able to keep our bodies under control. I think that James and Paul agreed based on Galatians 5:22-23.

> *the fruit of the Spirit is love, joy, peace, forbearance, kindness, goodness, faithfulness, gentleness and self-control.*

We are only able to keep our bodies under control and abstain from fleshly lust with wage war against our souls (1 Peter 2:11) as we are controlled by the Spirit of God.

Rendering control or dominion is an expression of worship. That's

one of the reasons that we can be sure that addictions are idols. Worship is expressed by making sacrifices to God (or a god), trusting, giving glory and praise, and allowing dominion.

But what is it that compels us, what motivates us to allow that dominion? It might be different for each individual. I have narrowed this down to three basic reasons for our submission (abstinence in this case.)

1. To avoid any negative consequences
2. To gain the benefits
3. Reverence (awe)

It's possible that we may desire just one or all of these at the same time. These elements can also be expressed in other words. To my knowledge, there are no other reasons why we do what we do (or don't do something.) Maturity is not obtainable without the fear of the Lord. There is no true sobriety without the fear of the Lord.

One of the very basics of spiritual maturity is reverence for the Almighty. In his letter to the Philippians, the apostle Paul exhorts believers to work out their own salvation with fear and trembling (reverence, Philippians 2:12). He, also, explains to the Corinthians how holiness is perfected through reverential fear (2 Corinthians 7:1). Why is reverence for God such an essential element of maturity? First, our relationship with God is determined by our reverence towards Him. Second, our integrity is governed by our reverence for God. Third, our relationship towards others depends on our reverence towards God.

Full or Empty

Blessed are those who hunger and thirst for righteousness, for they will be filled.
Matthew 5:6

Idolatrous addictions leave us empty. The very nature of idolatry is impractical. One of the definitions for an idol comes from the New Unger's Bible Dictionary. An idol is "an empty thing, rendered elsewhere 'trouble,' 'iniquity,' 'vanity,' 'wickedness,' etc. The primary idea of the root word seems to be emptiness, nothingness, as a breath or a vapor. The Hebrew word for idol (awen) denotes a vain, false, wicked thing and expresses at once the essential nature of idols and the consequences of their worth." Just like idols, addictions have an emptiness about them.

Jesus said to them, "I am the bread of life; whoever comes to me shall not hunger, and whoever believes in me shall never thirst." (John 6:35)

Be not silent! (part 1)

> *To You, O Lord, I call; my Rock, be not deaf to me, lest, if You be silent to me, I become like those who go down to the pit.*
> **Psalms 28:1**

I do not think that I alone have had times when I would foolishly stifle God if I could. (To be honest, there are still times I feel that way.) I thank Him that He mercifully forgives me of that. There were times during my drug addiction when such a rebellious attitude was very blatant.

I can remember when being faced with the opportunity of getting drugs with money that came unexpectedly. On more than one occasion, God was faithfully providing a way of escape beginning with reminding me of hymns that I had previously embraced. My response was to shut the memories of those hymns out of my head and literally say to God that I didn't want that and I was going to go get drugs. I am so very grateful for His mercy.

The last time that I chose to turn from the direction of God to the idolatry of drug addiction, the thing that I honestly feared the most was that God would never speak to me again. **Our lives are nothing without the Word of God**. Do you want proof? Look at the conditions of the world!

If it were not for the Word of God generating God-fearing people, this world would be in complete disorder and barbarism.

And I'm not just talking about society (as a whole.) We as individuals would each contribute to disorder as some already do by rejecting the Word of God.

There are many addictions (or habits) that plague our world today. Some of these addictions are old, others are new. The oldest and most hideous addiction is the root to all the others. That addiction is the systematic and consistent rejection of Jesus Christ. As a result, some of us down to the pit in this life, while others go to the pit in the next. All because we want God to be silent while He has spoken through His beloved Son.

Be not silent! (part 2)

*To You, O Lord, I call; my Rock, be not
deaf to me, lest, if you be silent to me, I
become like those who go down to the pit.*
Psalms 28:1

It sounds like a prayer of desperation. How
many times have we been there? And
sometimes we don't even want God's help in
times of desperation. Perhaps, you have heard
this joke before.

> A man named Jack was walking
> along a steep cliff one day when he
> accidentally got too close to the
> edge and fell. On the way down he
> grabbed a branch, which
> temporarily stopped his fall. He
> looked down and to his horror saw
> that the canyon fell straight down
> for more than a thousand feet.
>
> He couldn't hang onto the
> branch forever, and there was no
> way for him to climb up the steep
> wall of the cliff. So, Jack began
> yelling for help, hoping that
> someone passing by would hear
> him and lower a rope or something.

HELP! HELP! Is anyone up there?
"HELP!"
He yelled for a long time, but no one heard him. He was about to give up when he heard a voice. Jack, Jack. Can you hear me?"
"Yes, yes! I can hear you. I'm down here!"
"I can see you, Jack. Are you all right?"
"Yes, but who are you, and where are you?
"I am the Lord, Jack. I'm everywhere."
"The Lord? You mean, GOD?"
"That's Me."
"God, please help me! I promise if you'll get me down from here, I'll stop sinning. I'll be a really good person. I'll serve You for the rest of my life."
"Easy on the promises, Jack. Let's get you off from there; then we can talk."
"Now, here's what I want you to do. Listen carefully."
"I'll do anything, God. Just tell me what to do."
"Okay. Let go of the branch."
"What?" "I said, let go of the branch. Just trust Me. Let go."
There was a long silence.
Finally, Jack yelled, "HELP! HELP! IS ANYONE ELSE UP THERE?"

I am fully convinced that God has the answers to everything in His Word. I am finding out what God has to say about addictions at such an amazing rate that I cannot even keep track. Psalm 33:6 says, "By the Word of the Lord the heavens were made, and by the breath of His mouth all their host." Now, if He made the heavens by His Word, addictions don't stand a chance when His word is seriously applied. I am personally convinced that if the Word of God had nothing to say on addictions that God would not have created us!

Back to the issue of desperation. Edward T. Welch asks the following questions in his booklet concerning our attitude about sobriety.

• You want it, but without having to break a sweat.
• You want it because you are supposed to want it.
• You want it, but not at the cost of saying goodbye to something you love.
• You want it—sometimes
• You want it—tomorrow.
• You want it simply because it will make life a little easier or bring hope back to a relationship.
• You want it, but you are waiting for God to take away your cravings.

Desperation can be a weak motivation for seeking God if it is not coupled with sheer reverence for God.

Rest (part 1)

Come to Me, all who labor and are heavy laden, and I will give you rest. Take My yoke upon you, and learn from Me, for I am gentle and lowly in heart, and you will find rest for your souls. For My yoke is easy, and My burden is light.
Matthew 11:28-30

Rest is a tremendous aid to restoration. If we are to be restored into the people that God intended us to be then we must rest from our own works and engage in the work that God has for us. From there, we also rest from time to time as we are guided and instructed by the Master.

I once met a young man who was homeless, jobless and poorly educated. While attempting to meet with him to teach him some computer skills, he would never show up at our appointed time. On one occasion, after not seeing him for several weeks, I was hoping that he had begun to work on his situation. When I asked him what he had been doing, he said, "Taking it easy." When I asked, "Haven't you been doing that enough?", his response was, "You can never that it easy enough."

Needless to say, I do not agree with my friend's philosophy when it comes to making a living as well, as whatever other God-given responsibilities we are privileged. But addictions are not in God's plan. As a result, addictions are laborious. I cannot begin to tell you of all the work that I put into my addictions. Perhaps, you have some idea. And so, in this sense my friend was right. One thing that I have told people for years, whenever they have taken a break from their addiction is that it is easier to stay that way than to go back. This is what Ezra had in mind in the prayer recorded in Ezra 9:8.

> *But now for a brief moment favor has been shown by the Lord our God, to leave us a remnant and to give us a secure hold within His holy place, that our God may brighten our eyes and grant us a little reviving in our slavery.*

But, the most tremendous feature of resting is not that we cease from our own devices. Resting allows us to rejoice, rejoice in the Lord.

Rest (Part 2)

Woe to the multitude of many people, which make a noise like the noise of the seas; and to the rushing of nations, that make a rushing like the rushing of mighty waters! **Isaiah 17:12 KJV**

Does that sound like rest to you? Perhaps, our title should be unrest. This is a description of the multitudes who will not allow God to rule over their passions creating unrest. The unrest of many leads to addictions of various natures (some which are even sociably acceptable yet displeasing to God.)

I don't think that there is a soul alive that is not looking for rest. The question we must ask is where we are looking to find rest. It has been many years since I read *The Confession of St. Augustine*. Before I knew how famous the quote was, it had much value for me.

"Thou hast made us for Thyself, O Lord, and our heart is restless until it finds its rest in Thee."

As the return of Christ draws ever so near, we witness how mankind becomes more defiant than ever in shutting God out, producing unrest.

> *And there will be signs in sun and moon and stars, and on the earth distress of nations in perplexity because of the roaring of the sea and the waves,* **Luke 21:25**

In the Kingdom of God, there is rest because it is ruled by the Prince of Peace. There is no rest so long as we are ruled by addictions. There is no rest outside of the Kingdom of God.

High definition

> *The Lord passed before him and proclaimed, "The Lord, the Lord, a God merciful and gracious, slow to anger, and abounding in steadfast love and faithfulness, keeping steadfast love for thousands, forgiving iniquity and transgression and sin, but Who will by no means clear the guilty, visiting the iniquity of the fathers on the children and the children's children, to the third and the fourth generation."*
> **Exodus 34:6-7**

Look at how God is defined! This is high-definition from the Most High! While is tempting to comment upon each definition, I prefer to number them and then give you some descriptions for addiction in comparison. God says that He is:

1. A God merciful and gracious
2. Slow to anger
3. Abounding in steadfast love
4. Faithfulness
5. Keeping steadfast love
6. Forgiving
7. Will not clear the guilty
8. Visiting iniquity

Addictions are;

1. Lifeless idols
2. Unforgiving in their demands
3. Unfaithful
4. Conquerable
5. An idol is "an empty thing, rendered elsewhere 'trouble,' 'iniquity,' 'vanity,' 'wickedness,' etc. The primary idea of the root word seems to be emptiness, nothingness, as a breath or a vapor. The Hebrew

> word for idol (awen) denotes a
> vain, false, wicked thing and
> expresses at once the essential
> nature of idols and the
> consequences of their worth."
> (New Unger's Bible
> Dictionary)

As the years go by, I have gained more and more of an appreciation for the Word of God. Besides the power of Christ, I attribute my sobriety to an understanding and application of the Word of God. The introduction to every volume *Bible Verses Addictions* explains why the Word of God is so important while addressing addictions.

> "Another reason for a deeper
> study of the Word of God for
> addicts is to build up their faith.
> We who have been in the habit of
> putting our trust in an addiction,
> need to develop and maintain faith
> in God. Faith comes by hearing
> and hearing by the Word of God
> (Romans 10:17). As quiet as it is
> kept (though some may deny it)
> addicts have a small view of God.
> Addicts have trouble seeing how
> good God is. Addicts don't
> understand how merciful and

forgiving God is. Addicts have trouble believing that God has all power. It is because of this deficiency of faith that people lean upon their own understanding and put their trust in idolatrous addictions.

The written Word of God gives us the most accurate description there is of God. The most vivid description of God is found in the living Word of God (Jesus Christ, also described in the written Word of God). Another reason why the addict needs to have their faith built up by studying the Word of God is so that they can be on one accord with God as they pray.

A deeper study of the Word of God discloses and eradicates the deception and error on which addictions are rooted. Three basic areas of deceit that give addictions their strength is; the misinformation that they give concerning God, concerning ourselves, and the addiction (itself). Addictions discredit God. Addiction, basically, tell us that God is not to be trusted, He doesn't love us all that much, He doesn't know what He is talking about, we don't have to answer to Him (and many other lies, if we were to really think about it). The lies that are behind addictions concerning ourselves is that we know what is best, we are not all that bad, we can handle it (and again, many, many lies.")

Your Honor

The Lord descended in the cloud and stood with him there, and proclaimed the name of the Lord. **Exodus 34:5**

We have already established that there are three actions that God exhibits. The Lord descended. The Lord stood with Moses. And, the Lord proclaimed the name of the Lord. The first two actions communicate to us non-verbally. The third action is, clearly, verbal.

One of the ways we express ourselves is through words. This is an inheritance from God, as we were created in God's image. And so, God expresses Himself by word also. And the Word of God is more reliable than anything in all the universe. I like one of the definitions from the internet for "proclaim."

- declare something one considers important with due emphasis.

In Exodus 33:17 God tells Moses that He knows him. Now, in Exodus 34, God wants Moses to know Him. How important is it to know God? Does knowing God affect our view of addictions?

Let me suggest that the scene before us is as a courtroom where the Judge is about to arrive or in the announcement of a King's arrival. Is there anyone who knows God better than God? And so, God is best suited to herald His arrival.

As the Lord proclaims the name of the Lord, He is displaying His honor. As quiet as it is kept, this is what is most at stake when we succumb to addictions. In today's world, this is no longer a major concern. People are more worried about the effect that addictions have on themselves, families, society, etc. I am not saying that these are not important. One thing that I can guarantee is that if we are more concerned about God's honor, then He will take care of the rest!

The other limits

The Lord descended in the cloud and stood with him there, and proclaimed the name of the Lord. The Lord passed before him and proclaimed, "The Lord, the Lord, a God merciful and gracious, slow to anger, and abounding in steadfast love and faithfulness, keeping steadfast love for thousands, forgiving iniquity and transgression and sin, but Who will by no means clear the guilty, visiting the iniquity of the fathers on the children and the children's children, to the third and the fourth generation." **Exodus 34:5-7**

Perhaps you are old enough to remember a television program called *The Outer Limits*. At the introduction to the program, the announcer would beseech the viewers not to attempt to adjust their television because they were in control. Here are the exact words:

"There is nothing wrong with your television. Do not attempt to adjust the picture. We are now in control of the transmission. We control the horizontal and the vertical. We can deluge you with a thousand channels, or expand one single image to crystal clarity and beyond. We can shape your vision to anything our imagination can

conceive. For the next hour, we
will control all that you see and
hear."

Addictions try to convince us that there is
nothing wrong with our vision. God tells us
that there is. God is offering clear definition,
as with Moses (even more after the
presentation of His Son.) Addictions offer
distortion.

While it was my intention to comment on
Exodus 34: 5-7 in reference to addictions, I
came to realize that verses 1-16 have a lot to
say about addictions. Moses would not and
could not go on until God gave him vision.
Vision is what we need to overcome
addictions. Addictions hinder our view of
God, ourselves, others, and the addiction
(itself.) God, on the other hand, says, "my
thoughts are not your thoughts, neither are
your ways my ways... For as the heavens are
higher than the earth, so are my ways higher
than your ways and my thoughts than your
thoughts" (Isaiah 55:8-9).

One of the things that I can remember
about *The Outer Limits* is that each episode
could either be scary, undesirable, and
distasteful or pleasantly desirable. In either
case the episode would take you somewhere
you had never dreamed. Addictions take us to

the negative outer limits. God wants to take us to the more pleasant and desirable outer limits.

Hold it right there!

The Lord passed before him and proclaimed, "The Lord, the Lord, a God merciful and gracious, slow to anger, and abounding in steadfast love and faithfulness, keeping steadfast love for thousands, forgiving iniquity and transgression and sin, but Who will by no means clear the guilty, visiting the iniquity of the fathers on the children and the children's children, to the third and the fourth generation."
Exodus 34:6-7

What a sobering moment! Often within secular groups, it is said that a person will not give up their addiction until they reach their "bottom". The bottom for a follower of Christ should be their reverence for the Almighty! One thing that I can say beyond the shadow of a doubt is that so long as God has our attention then we will know how to deal with addictions.

The proclamation of God to Moses begins as the clear and intense call of attention to a soldier in the presence of a superior. Maybe, that is just one of the reasons that God begins by saying, "the Lord" twice. I can recall an experience where I received an intense call to attention in an unlikely manner by a complete stranger (unknowingly used of God.)

As I had, foolishly, decided at one point of my life that I would never try to quit using crack, I traveled to Florida where I thought that I could get the best crack in the country. I had developed a routine of visiting a homeless center several times a week after waking from a nearby hideout.

God was gracious and merciful in providing me with a "five-star" homeless center where I could eat breakfast, take a shower, get some fresh clean clothes and take a bag of food to go, despite my rebellion against the Lord.

After leaving the center I would spend the bulk of the day at a nearby college that allowed the public to use their computers. At one point in the day, I would go to a park just outside the library (located in an inlet to the Atlantic Ocean.) As, I fed the seagulls the scraps of food that I did not want, one of the college's staff approached. She started by saying, "I hope that you know what you are doing!". As she paused, my immediate thought was, "How does this woman know that I have given my life to crack?"

As I listened, I came to understand that the woman's concern was the reinforcement that I gave to the seagulls concerning the presence of food in the park. She said that when the seagulls know that there is food, they sometimes attack people.

God was reminding me that He is Lord and that my life is not my own. Although I did not quit using crack at that time, I am certain that it was those types of moments that have led to my 8 years of sobriety.

God was speaking to me at the park that day, as with other situations (both pleasant and unpleasant.) God spoke to Moses on the mount. The highest degree of sobriety is available as I stand at attention in response to my Commander the Lord, the Lord.

Delight in the Lord

*since it is written, "You shall be holy, for I am holy." **1 Peter 1:16 ESV***

The severest indictment that is not often mentioned concerning addictions is dissatisfaction with God. Oh, we don't say this out loud, but every time we engage in idolatrous addiction, we are saying that there is something wrong with God. The introduction to every volume of *Bible Verses Addiction* state that addictions discredit God.

"Addiction, basically, tells us that God is not to be trusted, He doesn't love us all that much, He doesn't know what He is talking about, we don't have to answer to Him (and many other lies, if we were to really think about it.)" For one thing, does not sin (especially idolatrous addictions) accuse God of being unreasonable?

God has manifest Himself most vividly in Christ. This is just one reason why a Christ-centered approach to addictions is essential. Without Jesus we do not have a complete view of God nor can we be friends with Him. Those who really know me have heard me say time and time again that "the highest degree of sobriety is in Jesus Christ."

Don't you think that being close friends with God could extinguish our lust for addictions? Do you think that if we delight ourselves in God that it would cause us to be less inclined to delight in addictions? Do you think that God is worthy of such? This is what is primarily seen in 1 Peter 1:16 concerning addictions. Furthermore, the glory of God comes must always, always come first in our treatment of addictions.

Reserved/preserved

"All things are lawful for me," but not all things are helpful. "All things are lawful for me," but I will not be dominated by anything. **1 Corinthians 6:12**

As quiet as it's kept, if we do not deal with each and everything that we know to be offensive to God then we do not hear His voice as well. As a result of not hearing His voice so well we become vulnerable to drifting from the safety that He affords. If we continue to engage in certain behavior (outside of our primary addiction), it may eventually lead us back.

Not only does the addict have to give up every addiction that is displeasing to God, but they may also have to give up some things that are not addictive within themselves yet associated with their addiction(s). There may be things that remind them of their addiction, there may be people that they must not associate with (at least not so closely, in some cases not at all.) Just think of how Abram was called by God to leave his homeland because of their idolatry. God wanted him all to Himself. The same is true for you. And He worthy.

National security

*When new gods were chosen, then war was
in the gates. Was shield or spear to be seen
among forty thousand in Israel?*
Judges 5:8 ESV

The security of Israel was threatened because
of their idolatry just as it had been foretold in
Deuteronomy 32.

> *"But Jeshurun grew fat, and kicked;*
> *you grew fat, stout, and sleek;*
> *then he forsook God who made him*
> *and scoffed at the Rock of his salvation.*
> *They stirred him to jealousy with strange
> gods;*
> *with abominations they provoked him to
> anger.*
> *They sacrificed to demons that were no gods,*
> *to gods they had never known,*
> *to new gods that had come recently,*
> *whom your fathers had never dreaded.*
> *You were unmindful of the Rock that
> bore[e] you,*
> *and you forgot the God who gave you birth.*
> *"The Lord saw it and spurned them,*
> *because of the provocation of his sons and
> his daughters.*
> *And he said, 'I will hide my face from them;*

> *I will see what their end will be,*
> *for they are a perverse generation,*
> *children in whom is no faithfulness.*
> ***vv. 15-20 ESV***

Israel had become unequipped to face her challenges because of her idolatry. Just as Israel, we become declassified as a result of addictions (to say the least.)

Promotion vs. Demotion

> *Should I leave my wine, which cheereth God and man, and go to be promoted over the trees?* ***Judges 9:13 KJV***

Addictions are beneath you. You were created to be a reflection unto God and of the greatest possible use to others. In the verse above we are given a portion of a parable by Jotham. It is the irony of an invitation given to the grapevine to rule over the trees. The grapevine's response is that she was created for something better. What is said to be a promotion would be a demotion.

And so it is with the call of addictions inviting us to rule. The response that God has given to us is that we were created for something better. While addictions appear to be a promotion on the surface, they are a demotion.

Trained

Blessed are those whose way is blameless,
who walk in the law of the Lord!
Psalms 119:1 ESV

It is said that walking is good exercise. I would have to say that it depends on where you are walking. If you are walking in the direction of a cliff, it would not be a good exercise to continue walking in the same direction. Walking is often used in Scripture to describe the way that we live. I was fascinated by all the implications behind walking and living as I studied for the publication of *The Fear of the Almighty*. Some of the phrases that I found are:

1. Walk in His law
2. The way wherein they must walk
3. Neither shall ye walk in their ordinances (Canaan)
4. Keep mine ordinances, to walk

therein

5. Walk contrary unto me
6. Walk after other gods
7. Walk after the imagination of his evil heart
8. Walk in lies
9. Walk in darkness
10. Walk in the newness of life
11. Walk in the Spirit
12. Walk by faith
13. Walk in the flesh
14. Walk after the flesh
15. Walk in love
16. Walk circumspectly
17. Walk in truth
18. Walk as He walked
19. Walk in the light
20. Walking in the fear of God

Walking can be defined as a practice as well. As I have practiced exercising for three days a week for the last eight years, I am pleased with how far I have come. (I think that God is pleased as well) As I practiced using crack for 23 intermittent years, I was not pleased with the results. More importantly, God was not pleased. The most distinguishable thing about a walk is the direction it leads. It has been said that we are either walking toward God or walking away from Him. A walk eventually accumulates distance. Just start walking, and before you know, you have travelled a distance. That's how addictions get us into trouble. But, for all that it's worth- our walk is a daily walk. **"Sin will take you farther than you want to go, keep you longer than you want to stay, and cost you more than you want to pay."**

Many argue that the Scriptures don't say anything about addictions. I beg to differ. The world wants to free us of our guilt by saying that sin does not exist rather than looking to Jesus. The Scriptures clearly state that some things are godly and others are ungodly. Addictions are ungodly. Two passages that make a distinction between the walk that addictions invite us to *and* the walk that Christ invites us are Ephesians 2:1-3 and 1 Timothy 4:7 (ESV).

And you were dead in the trespasses and sins in which you once walked, following the course of this world, following the prince of the power of the air, the spirit that is now at work in the sons of disobedience— among whom we all once lived in the passions of our flesh, carrying out the desires of the body and the mind, and were by nature children of wrath, like the rest of mankind.

> *Have nothing to do with*
> *irreverent, silly myths. Rather train*
> *yourself for godliness; for*
> *while bodily training is of some*
> *value, godliness is of value in every*
> *way, as it holds promise for the*
> *present life and also for the life to*
> *come.*
> *(The KJV uses the word "exercise"*
> *rather than train)*

Training well describes the process that God wants to perform in our war against addictions. I love the implications that are brought forth in Psalms 18:34.

> *He trains my hands for war so that*
> *my arms can bend a bow of bronze.*

Concluding

Repentance leading to transformation

For if we have been united with Him in a death like His, we shall certainly be united with Him in a resurrection like His.
Romans 6:5 (ESV)

In conclusion, I must state the obvious fact that for the process of sobriety to take full effect we must be born again, saved, united with Christ **(all describing the same act of God that takes place when our sins are forgiven and the bridge between us and God is removed.) Without this occurrence, there is not much communication between God and us**.

Another thing that I must mention is that the process that is being described most certainly can be described in other words and contains other elements that may not be mentioned. For instance, self-denial is within this process. Fasting is highly recommended. Prayer is essential for sobriety as well as many other features that have not been mentioned.

The transformation that takes place makes us as human as Jesus is (though He was also God, a mystery.) One of the most valuable lessons that I learned in a class on the doctrine of Christ is that Jesus was more human than anyone that has ever lived.

The truth of the matter is that addictions cause us to think and behave like animals. The fact that addictions cause us to think and behave as animals can be seen on so many levels. Animals tend to be unreasonable- addicts tend to be unreasonable.

The blessed transformation that Almighty God brings about as we repent (change our minds about sin, about ourselves, about Jesus) is described in 2 Corinthians 3:18

And we all, with unveiled face, beholding the glory of the Lord, are being transformed into the same image from one degree of glory to another. For this comes from the Lord who is the Spirit.

Bibliography

Brother Lawrence, *The Practice of the Presence of God*, trans. John Delaney (Image, 1977)

Confessions of St. Augustine

Gifford, John, *Pilgrims Progress (preface, 1678)*

Lockyer, Herbert, *All the Divine Names and Titles in the Bible* (Zondervan, 1975)

MacArthur, John, *Hard to Believe* (2010, Thomas Nelson)

Mack, Wayne A., *The Distinguishing Feature of Christian Counseling* (article)

Madison, Gregory, *Turning to God from Idols* (Awe of My Life Publications, 2018)

Narcotics Anonymous

New Unger Bible Dictionary

Niebuhr, Reinhold, *The Serenity Prayer*

Pink, A.W., quote

Powlinson, David, *Idols of the Heart and "Vanity Fair"* (article)

Pearce, Donn, and Pierson, Frank, *Cool Hand Luke* (screenplay, 1967)

Venning, Ralph, *The Sinfulness of Sin* (The Banner of Truth Trust, 1965)

Welch, Edward T., *Addictions: A Banquet in the Grave* (P&R Publishing, 2001)

Welch, Edward T., *Just One More* (P&R Publishing, 2002)

More of a Biblical approach to addictions available by visiting the following:

Awe of My Life Publications
www.turningtogodfromidols.com

Bible Verses Addictions (Study):
www.facebook.com/groups/bibleversesaddictions

High Sobriety Society
https://www.facebook.com/groups/thebestanswer/

Awe of My Life
https://www.facebook.com/praisetofightaddictions/

Quality Christian Resources on Addictions
www.facebook.com/groups/jesusbringssobriety/

Thanks for reading! If you enjoyed this book or found it useful, I'd be very grateful if you'd post a short review on Amazon. Your support really does make a difference and I read all the reviews personally so I can get your feedback and make this book even better.

Bible Verses Addictions and bears the philosophy concerning addictions that are found in ***Turning to God from Idols: A Biblical Approach to Addictions b***y Gregory Madison.

Books by Gregory Madison include:

Turning to God from Idols
Sobriety for Christmas
Bible Verses Addictions
(series, plain and illustrated)
The Fear of the Almighty
(all available on Amazon)

Visit our website for a preview of our books!
www.turningtoGodfromidols.com